Reformation of the Nations
(Manual for Kingdom Advance)

*Ebook*

Douglas Cameron Bailey
Rhona Bailey

Copyright © 2009 - 2013 Tehillah Apostolic Network

Published by Tehillah Publications

All rights reserved . No portion of this book may be reproduced in any form without the written permission of the publisher .

ISBN-13: 978-1900993067

Unless otherwise indicated , all scripture quotations are taken from the Holy Bible ,

Authorised King James Version .

Tehillah Publications
25 Cotswold Gardens
East Ham
London
E6 3HZ

United Kingdom

# Reformation of the Nations
## (Manual for Kingdom Advance)

## Contents

| | |
|---|---|
| About this Manual | 3 |
| A. Introduction to Reformation | 4 |
| B. Reformation | 6 |
| C. Design of Structure | 8 |
| D. Ministers | 10 |
| E. Kingdoms | 11 |
|    I. Home/Family | 12 |
|    II. Church/Faith | 14 |
|    III. Government/Politics | 15 |
|    IV. Business, Economy, Science and Technology | 16 |
|    V. Education | 17 |
|    VI. Media and Communication | 18 |
|    VII. Arts, Entertainment and Sports | 19 |
| F. God's Reformers | 20 |
| G. Kingdom Ways, Keys and Principles | 36 |
| H. Kingdom Principles from Kingdom Reformers | 43 |
| Apostolic Transition (Synopsis) | 46 |
| Registration Form | 51 |
| Training & Contact Details | 53 |

# Reformation of the Nations
## (Manual for Kingdom Advance)

## About this Manual

### Purpose
The Supreme, Sovereign, Lord God Almighty - Jehovah is orchestrating a mighty reformation upon planet earth to advance the kingdom of Heaven. The purpose of this manual is to help those who support what the LORD is doing and to be able to posture themselves to come into an accurate partnership with the divine master plan. True son-ship is coming into accurate relationship and partnership with God through Jesus Christ.

### Overview
Reformation of the nations is an ongoing topic and like revelation is a progressive topic on the agenda of heaven for earth. This manual is the release of material compiled by the Holy Spirit.

This is present truth, currently revealed truth, of God's kingdom purpose on earth in this hour.

In order to function accurately we need to work with what God is doing and support His grand destiny for earth to quicken Christ's coming and release preparation for Christ's millennial reign and end-time events.

### Application
Like any information for it to become an instrument of change it has to have those who will receive the information and then apply the information into real life situations. It is hoped that this manual will be accepted by ministries who are not happy with the state of their respective nations and who really want to come into a greater more effective relationship with Almighty God to bring reform into the nations for kingdom advance.

### Prayer
I call forth in the name of Jesus the reformers in the Church who will rise up and be awakened in revelation and burden to reach out to the nations with this kingdom mandate. To release all that the Spirit of God is speaking to the nations for kingdom advance in this hour. Go forth with zeal and uncompromising faith to reach into the heart of the nations to see God's kingdom come in earth's systems as it is in heaven. We thank you Father.

# Reformation of the Nations
## (Manual for Kingdom Advance)

### A. Introduction to Reformation

**1. Revelation 11:15 (Amplified Bible)**

"The seventh angel then blew [his] trumpet, and there were mighty voices in heaven, shouting, The dominion (kingdom, sovereignty, rule) of the world has now come into the possession and become the kingdom of our Lord and of His Christ (the Messiah), and He shall reign forever and ever (for the eternities of the eternities)!"

From our opening text we can see that the word of God is emphatic about reinforcing the victory and
dominion of Jesus Christ bringing all the kingdoms in this world system under the direct influence and
control of heaven. Indeed from the book of Genesis, the seedbed of God's declared purposes, we can see that the dominion mandate is relevant for our study of reformation. The original design plan was laid out .

**2. Genesis 1:28 (Amplified Bible)**

"And God blessed them and said to them, Be fruitful, multiply, and fill the earth, and subdue it [using all its vast resources in the service of God and man]; and have dominion over the fish of the sea, the birds of the air, and over every living creature that moves upon the earth."

The question is how do we , the Church , partner with God to effectively advance the kingdom of heaven in earth's systems. Jesus taught us how to pray in the Lord's prayer but what is contained within this teaching is very interesting .

**3. Matthew 6:10 (Amplified Bible)**

"Your kingdom come, Your will be done on earth as it is in heaven. "

We have here a direct statement of a future promise. This is decree spoken in place by the Lord Himself. This shall take place but we don't know exactly when. Decrees are very important when studying God's promises contained in His plans.

### 4. Job 22:28
**"Thou shalt also decree a thing, and it shall be established unto thee: and the light shall shine upon thy ways."**

*Decree - (Hebrew - gazar) to cut down or off, to divide, exclude, decide; it is an executive command which legislates. It becomes imperative (urgent, extremely important or urgent; needing to be done or given attention immediately:)*

From our text we can see that once the decree is released which is in agreement with God's will our
foundation is laid and the result will be a firm place to function. Once that place is established increased revelation will follow. This becomes the place for increased divine strategy to flow into our life situations. When decrees are mixed with the word of God there are going to be some promises fulfilled. There is no question about it.
It is a done deal !
Having established that a superior righteous kingdom is going to be over all other kingdoms it is now our mission of life to find out how we as the Church can be used by God to bring this decree to a closer place. In reality we are not going to see all sin eradicated, all wars cease and social depravation cleaned up until after the millennial reign of Christ.

### 5. Revelation 20:4-5 (Amplified Bible)
**"Then I saw thrones, and sitting on them were those to whom authority to act as judges and to pass sentence was entrusted. Also I saw the souls of those who had been slain with axes [beheaded] for their witnessing to Jesus and [for preaching and testifying] for the Word of God, and who had refused to pay homage to the beast or his statue and had not accepted his mark or permitted it to be stamped on their foreheads or on their hands. And they lived again and ruled with Christ (the Messiah) a thousand years. The remainder of the dead were not restored to life again until the thousand years were completed. This is the first resurrection "**

In the meantime however as the Church we can be instruments in God's hands to bring an increasing influence over the kingdoms of this world.

Our introduction has set out the main areas of discussion to help us understand what God is requiring of each of us who are related to Him. He wants all of His family to come to a closer working relationship with Him so that He can express His kingdom through our lives. That means our lives 24/7 and 365 days per year and anywhere and everywhere. This is our mandate and commission to demonstrate His kingdom here on earth as it is in heaven. ( this topic is explored under " Kingdoms " page 5 )

## B. Reformation

### 1. So what is Reformation ?

The only direct scriptural reference is found in **Hebrews 9:10** when the writer of Hebrews was discussing the old testament activities of sacrifice to provide a way of covering sin. " Time of Reformation " was the divinely appointed time when Jesus our high priest , the lamb of sacrifice was to enter once only into the very presence of God to fulfil all that is required for sin to be fully paid for. **Hebrews 9:11.**

**Hebrews 9:10-11 (Amplified Bible)**

**"For [the ceremonies] deal only with clean and unclean meats and drinks and different washings, [mere] external rules and regulations for the body imposed to tide the worshipers over until the time of setting things straight [of reformation, of the complete new order when Christ, the Messiah, shall establish the reality of what these things foreshadow--a better covenant].**
**But [that appointed time came] when Christ (the Messiah) appeared as a High Priest of the better things that have come and are to come. [Then] through the greater and more perfect tabernacle not made with [human] hands, that is, not a part of this material creation,"**

2. This time of reformation was Christ coming to replace the old with the new. Old ordinances of ritual sacrifice with animals and animal blood was being made redundant and a new and better way established. That's contained in reformation – it is the bringing back of something in it's existing state to the original design state. Returning it to the manufacturers original design criteria so that it will function according to design. Our text in **Genesis 1:28** shares this same vision of what God had set as His design from the very beginning.

Basically , sin got in the way and has continued to do so. This sin in every strata of society which we also call kingdoms has laid the way for total dysfunctional activity opposed to righteous kingdom principles and values as set by the Lord himself.

3. Another aspect of reformation is restitution which is referred to in **Acts 3:21** .

**Acts 3:21**
**"Whom the heaven must receive until the times of restitution of all things, which God hath spoken by the mouth of all his holy prophets since the world began."**

Again this is referring to a future event of the time when Christ returns to earth to set up His millennial kingdom.

*Restitution (Greek apokatastasis ) reconstitute in health , home or organisation ,restore again.*

Restitution is the putting together of all it's components into a specific designed order to enable a set of conditions to be satisfied. It is returning something back to original design. Restitution contains several activities in the pursuit of it's goal of original design. These are reformation, revival and reconstitution.

*Reformation (Greek: diorthosis) is returning back to design by reordering it's internal structure and mechanisms to affect the outer model or function.*

4. Inner structural overhaul of mentality, understanding, learned behaviours, culture and tradition, attitudes and perceptions have to be made in order for the fresh value systems of this present reformation to be accurately reflected to the outside world by the Church.
This is commonly known collectively as the "Paradigm Shift"

This is the essential substance that must change in order for the outer model the "kingdom of God within" to be effectively demonstrated to the world. Unless the world sees a better system consistently demonstrated they will not be influenced one bit ! This is our mandate from God in this hour . It will mean fully understanding , grasping and catching what the kingdom of heaven here on earth is all about. That's the true reformation that God is presently releasing into the earth and especially within His Church as the instrument of change !

It's not a matter of "are we ready ?" but simply be ready and NOW !
It's God's highest plan for us today !

**5. Revival** is the activity of putting life back into something that was dead.

*Revive (Hebrew chayah) to live , keep ,make alive , preserve alive, quicken , recover, repair ,*
*restore to life , save , be whole .*

Reconstitution is placing various assigned components back into an order that produces the original design parameters. Mashed potatoes in the form of powder when treated with hot water becomes the substance we can consume.

## C. Design of structure

1. We have established that there is an activity going on conducted by the Lord Himself from heaven to see His kingdom come in earth as it is in heaven. He has also declared to His Church that they would be the primary instrument in His hand to advance His kingdom. He spoke this and commissioned us all as the Church from what we call the "Great Commission "

## Matthew 28:18-20

"And Jesus came and spake unto them, saying, All power is given unto me in heaven and in earth.

Go ye therefore, and teach all nations, baptizing them in the name of the Father, and of the Son, and of the Holy Ghost: Teaching them to observe all things whatsoever I have commanded you: and, lo, I am with you always, even unto the end of the world. Amen."

*Power (Greek - exousia)*
*force,capacity,competency,freedom,mastery,superhuman,potentate,token of control,delegated,influence,authority upon, jurisdiction,liberty,power,right,strength.*

*Nations (Greek - ethnos) a race, a tribe, of the same habit, people*

2. So here we see that we have a commission to go into all nations, ethnos peoples groups – all strata of society and do something !
That something is to teach these nations to follow Christ's teaching about His kingdom.
Christ's teaching, that which He spoke and that which He demonstrated is what constitutes the value system of the kingdom of heaven.
Jesus is of course the king of the kingdom and anything He said or did makes up the way that His kingdom functions. It is that kingdom that is being released through the Church today. Our function then is to understand how we can effectively demonstrate His superior kingdom.

3. Teaching involves not only telling people facts but demonstrating them. Holy Spirit was released from heaven to be with us in this function. He empowers us with spiritual gifts. They are not for goose bumps and spectacular fireworks but for very practical demonstration of what heaven's kingdom operates through. Where we live, where we work, where we study – for kingdom advance

The marketplace and workplace are where we live and work and study.
This place is where we all at some time function in one role or another.

## D. Ministers
1. We could call this our place of primary ministry. Does that mean we are all ministers?
Yes we are all ministers but not all fivefold or governmental ministers.

**Isaiah 61:6 (Amplified Bible)**

"But you shall be called the priests of the Lord; people will speak of you as the ministers of our God. You shall eat the wealth of the nations, and the glory [once that of your captors] shall be yours."

**Ephesians 4:11 (Amplified Bible)**

"And His gifts were [varied; He Himself appointed and gave men to us] some to be apostles (special messengers), some prophets (inspired preachers and expounders), some evangelists (preachers of the Gospel, traveling missionaries), some pastors (shepherds of His flock) and teachers."

Minister is simply a term meaning a servant or worker.

*Minister - (Greek diakonos) waiter, one who waits on or serves others.*

## 2. Character
We influence our way into these earthly realms by our lifestyle and our Godly character. See the text below to see the example of Christ as not only the very image of God but also having the same character.

**Hebrews 1:3 (Amplified Bible)**

"He is the sole expression of the glory of God [the Light-being, the out-raying or radiance of the divine], and He is the perfect imprint and very image of [God's] nature, upholding and maintaining and guiding and propelling the universe by His mighty word of power. When He had by offering Himself accomplished our cleansing of sins and riddance of guilt, He sat down at the right hand of the divine Majesty on high."

It is therefore essential that we function by depending upon the Holy Spirit within us and not on our own carnality.

**Romans 12** tells us that we are of the spirit if we be connected to God . We must walk in the spirit and not the flesh . There is no kingdom worth in the flesh but in the spirit. This is an essential **key** to function from for the kingdom of God in earth .

*Character - (Greek charaktēr, from charasse ) to scratch, engrave; Usage: when a character is used to stamp a soft material it leaves a perfect image of the character. It is the same as we follow Christ as the true character we too will look like Him. This is what character is all about , taking on the same image as the master character.*

*Carnal - (Greek sarkikos ) having the nature of flesh.. i.e. sensual, controlled by animal and base appetites, governed by human nature instead of by the Spirit of God.*

**E. Kingdoms**

1. What are the kingdoms of this world that will become the kingdoms of our Lord and of His Christ ?
Many call these so-called kingdoms , spheres of influence, social segments , gateways , seats of power etc...

Firstly what is a kingdom ?
*(Hebrew - mamlakah) (Greek - Basileia)*

Dominion , empire , estate , country, realm, king's reign + royal , royalty , rule, realm , foundation of power, sovereign .

**Summarising :**

*It is the territory that belongs and is controlled by the sovereign ruler.*
In every society there are 7 spheres of influence:

   I.   Home/Family
   II.  Church/Faith
   III. Government/Politics
   IV.  Business, Economy, Science and Technology
   V.   Education
   VI.  Media and Communication
   VII. Arts. Entertainment and Sports

There has to be a functioning process in place to release kingdom influence in all these seven spheres or kingdoms. This process must have an interface a method and carriers of this kingdom influence.

The Church is that carrier because we already carry the king and His kingdom within us the moment we are born again. It is interesting to consider the various ways we the Church can influence these kingdoms. These are a collection of ways that are presently being released in these kingdoms :

**I. Home/Family**

Bible believing families where Jesus is the head of the home. Where the home has a family altar and worship of God is as much the lifestyle as it is a specific times of intimacy as a family. From this foundation God sends the family out into the community and nations to demonstrate His kingdom.

There is Godly order in the structure of the home so that kingdom values are upheld and promoted.

Ephesians 5:22-28 (The Message)

"Wives, understand and support your husbands in ways that show your support for Christ. The husband provides leadership to his wife the way Christ does to his church, not by domineering but by cherishing. So just as the church submits to Christ as he exercises such leadership, wives should likewise submit to their husbands. Husbands, go all out in your love for your wives, exactly as Christ did for the church—a love marked by giving, not getting. Christ's love makes the church whole. His words evoke her beauty. Everything he does and says is designed to bring the best out of her, dressing her in dazzling white silk, radiant with holiness. And that is how husbands ought to love their wives. They're really doing themselves a favor—since they're already "one" in marriage. "

Ephesians 6:1-4 (The Message)

"Children, do what your parents tell you. This is only right. "Honor your father and mother" is the first commandment that has a promise attached to it, namely, "so you will live well and have a long life. Fathers, don't exasperate your children by coming down hard on them. Take them by the hand and lead them in the way of the Master."

## II. Church/Faith

Kingdom focused where the mind of Christ is functioning - Apostolic & Prophetic present truth revelation is taught and reproduced. Relevant kingdom expression to the community. Where Eph.4:11-16 is being taught, caught and manifest. The Saints are being equipped and released to the nations with the gospel of the kingdom.

**Ephesians 4:11-16 (Amplified Bible)**

"And His gifts were [varied; He Himself appointed and gave men to us] some to be apostles (special messengers), some prophets (inspired preachers and expounders), some evangelists (preachers of the Gospel, traveling missionaries), some pastors (shepherds of His flock) and teachers. His intention was the perfecting and the full equipping of the saints (His consecrated people), [that they should do] the work of ministering toward building up Christ's body (the church), [That it might develop] until we all attain oneness in the faith and in the comprehension of the [full and accurate] knowledge of the Son of God, that [we might arrive] at really mature manhood (the completeness of personality which is nothing less than the standard height of Christ's own perfection), the measure of the stature of the fullness of the Christ and the completeness found in Him. So then, we may no longer be children, tossed [like ships] to and fro between chance gusts of teaching and wavering with every changing wind of doctrine, [the prey of] the cunning and cleverness of unscrupulous men, [gamblers engaged] in every shifting form of trickery in inventing errors to mislead. Rather, let our lives lovingly express truth [in all things, speaking truly, dealing truly, living truly]. Enfolded in love, let us grow up in every way and in all things into Him Who is the Head, [even] Christ (the Messiah, the Anointed One). For because of Him the whole body (the church, in all its various parts), closely joined and firmly knit together by the joints and ligaments with which it is supplied, when each part [with power adapted to its need] is working properly [in all its functions], grows to full maturity, building itself up in love.

## III. Government & Politics

Christian members of Parliament and Christian Parties that release the truth of the word and function with integrity, justice , judgement and equity for all spheres of society, particularly social justice. God's laws are written in God-fearing men and women and they express kingdom values and character in the laws of the land . National and local government is highly influenced by these chosen Saints.

*Social Justice - Provision of social based needs including housing , employment , education and*
*support both financial and advice being made available to all segments of society particularlly those with dependency issues including, alcoholism, drug abuse , ex offenders and migrant communities.*

**Proverbs 1:1-3 (King James Version)**

"The proverbs of Solomon the son of David, king of Israel; To know wisdom and instruction; to perceive the words of understanding; To receive the instruction of wisdom, justice, and judgment, and equity;"

*Integrity - (Hebrew tom,tummah ) completeness, simplicity, upright , to be whole*

*Justice - (Hebrew tsedeq) the right , equity , altogether just and right*

*Judgment - (Hebrew mishpat) a verdict pronounced judicially , a sentence or formal decree , determination , charge , statutory order, ordinance*

*Equity - (Hebrew meyshar) evenness, prosperity , concord , agreement , aright , that are equal ,*
*sweetly , upright*

## IV. Business, Economy, Science and Technology

Applying the strategies obtained from the Lord and from His word. Functioning with kingdom character which means following as Christ's disciples within the workplace and marketplace.

### Strategy ( Greek strategia)

A plan of action resulting from strategy or intended to accomplish a specific goal . In military terms , how a battle is fought is a matter of <u>tactics</u>: whether there should be a fight is a matter of <u>strategy.</u>

This produces trust and honour and results in business with equity and fairness.
Just like Joseph in the times of famine will produce resources which have been stored up for this season of lack.

### Genesis 41:56 (King James Version)

"And the famine was over all the face of the earth: and Joseph opened all the storehouses, and sold unto the Egyptians; and the famine waxed sore in the land of Egypt."

In God there is no lack because He is the king and is able to meet all our need.

### Phil.4:19
"But my God shall supply all your need according to his riches in glory by Christ Jesus."

### Eph.3:20
"Now unto him that is able to do exceeding abundantly above all that we ask or think, according to the power that worketh in us,"

The kingdom of God is a superior kingdom and is able to provide in all areas of need. God is the ultimate creator and when we access His system of technology we can apply it within the world's systems of technology. He made man with a fine mind . It is when that mind is submitted to kingdom values through spiritual rebirth that the mind of Christ , the king , becomes ours to function effectively in whatever environment we are in. That's the demonstration of this superior kingdom in action.

**Prov.8:12** "Proverbs 8:12 (King James Version)

"I wisdom dwell with prudence, and find out knowledge of witty inventions."

We have access to this technology through God's wisdom !

*Wisdom ( Hebrew chokmah) skilful , intelligent , deal wisely*
*The application of knowledge with understanding*

*Prudence ( Hebrew ermah) discretion, guile, subtilty , wisdom*

*Knowledge (Hebrew da'ath)*
*comprehension,discernment,understanding,awareness , be learned , acquisition of facts*

## V. Education -
**Prov.22:6** "train up a child in the way he should go and when he is old he will not depart from it"

*Train (Hebrew chanak) discipline by teaching*

Training has the function of imparting knowledge and then giving the opportunity to apply that knowledge . It involves teaching,equipping,activating,mentoring and sending into the world for kingdom purpose. Even though a young student attends an education establishment that does not primarily promote biblical principles , these are formed in the foundation of the godly life of the student and they are able to make godly decisions about their education. Psychology and sociology for instance teach things which are derived from their understanding of the world's way of perceiving how the mind works and how society should function. Understanding and applying the value system of the kingdom of God throughout will ensure accuracy in alignment with the king. Here the principle that we have stewardship of the earth and it's systems given us by the king in **Gen.1:28** is applied . So even though we are in the world we are certainly not of it. We come from a different place when we are born again. We have become kingdom citizens and function under the constitution of that kingdom which is the word of God.

**VI. Media** - This is the communication by every means to ascertain facts and then present them to the public for opinion to be formed. The world has a vested interest in showing the facts in certain ways depending upon their political viewpoint. The left eye see things differently from the right eye . This is how the world operates with partial truth . Remember a partial truth is a whole lie. Ultimately there is only one truth and that is Christ , the king.

Jesus said in :

**John 14:6**

**" I am the way,the truth and the life no man comes to the Father except by me"**
**So Jesus is the truth .**

Media that is based on the Word will always see the truth through the eyes of the Word. They will have kingdom perception , seeing things as the king sees them , that sees the reality of a situation and also has the keys to resolve that situation. This is really the application and activation of the mind of Christ

**1 Corinthians 2:16 (Amplified Bible)**

**"For who has known or understood the mind (the counsels and purposes) of the Lord so as to guide and instruct Him and give Him knowledge? But we have the mind of Christ (the Messiah) and do hold the thoughts (feelings and purposes) of His heart."**

## VII. Arts. Entertainment and Sports

The film industry is being reformed by those God is raising up with His creative,innovative ideas that portray His character , His never ending creativity and His superior righteous values. These ones are being mentored by the Holy Spirit at this very moment , passionately working in His secret place waiting for the moment when He will release the full productive resources to enable that grand moment of release . This release will usher in the greatest reformation of the film industry that the world has ever seen. It will tower over Hollywood and be used by God to draw the people to Himself by the millions ! People will once again see the righteous values of life and compare them with the soiled values of the world. They will choose what the Lord is shining forth . They will be drawn to the light !

Sports will once again demonstrate kingdom principles of fair play. Players will not outburst with fleshly behaviour but righteous, godly character will be seen . Professional sportsmen have become business players and are paid enormous sums of money . They have become saleable items to go from one team to another by the directives of professional sports organisations . This has brought great disrepute into the games arena .This games arena has been existing ever since man competed against man and seen very much in the Roman amphitheatres. Then it was to the death but today it is not to death but is close in the attitudes and behaviour of the players who lose the ball or are fouled .God is raising up young players with personal integrity who through their obvious dependence upon Him and His word will demonstrate righteous behaviour . This will be as much off the field as on the field.

2.The Word describes this atmosphere of greed, covetness and mamom (love of money) .

### 1 Timothy 3:3 (Amplified Bible)

**"Not given to wine, not combative but gentle and considerate, not quarrelsome but forbearing and peaceable, and not a lover of money [insatiable for wealth and ready to obtain it by questionable means]."**

From all these brief excursions into these seven spheres or kingdoms one thing is gradually coming forth from one level to the next in increasing power. It is what the Lord said in His Word.

**Hab.2:14**
**"For the earth shall be filled with the knowledge of the glory of the Lord , as the waters cover the sea."**

It is part of the unfolding process of releasing the kingdom of God into earth's systems as it is in heaven and bringing the earth to a pre-determined place where God will release Jesus the king to come back to earth to set up His millennial kingdom when we shall see the ultimate purity of this righteous kingdom in action. Not only shall we see it , we shall be part of it !
We can begin to be part of it now in this realm and dispensation with our un-glorified bodies to usher in the Lord back to earth. We are demonstrators of this kingdom because this kingdom is a spiritual kingdom and is within us .

**Luke 17:21**
**" Neither shall they say to you , See here ; or , lo there ! For , behold , the kingdom of God is within you."**

**F.God's Reformers**

1.We as the family of God are the reformers of the nations , the instrument of change in the earth .
This is not a new phenomenon but has existed throughout earth's history . Men and women have been
chosen by God to manifest His personal character and values to the surrounding world to demonstrate His superior ways .
Let us explore the character and function of a reformer
We saw from our study of the definition of reformation that it is changing something back from it's existing state to the original designed state to accomplish the design standards and function.

A reformer then is a person who through their commitment to the originating design value , gives themselves up to serve this superior standard of living . They go against public opinion not to be offensive but simply to advance the ideals they have had imparted into their being . They are so infused with the rightness of what they believe that they don't count their life unto death . They think more of what they believe than their own lives. They contain the substance that makes martyrs. Like Jesus and David they have a heart after the heart of God.

**Revelation 12:11 (Amplified Bible)**

**11And they have overcome (conquered) him by means of the blood of the Lamb and by the utterance of their testimony, for they did not love and cling to life even when faced with death [holding their lives cheap till they had to die for their witnessing].**

**2.These are some of the historical reformers who God used :**

**Moses , Joshua , Abraham , Joseph , Nehemiah , David , Deborah , Esther , Ruth , Daniel , Elijah , Paul , Stephen , Jesus .**

We will briefly look into each of these great biblical characters and discover some of the things they did and what those things constitute as a kingdom reforming act.

We want to learn from these ones who went before us so we can emulate their character , commitment and faith .

We have to be able to do what they did by faith in the one who they believed in.

The earth shall be changed and we shall make a difference in Jesus name !

---

**Consecration Prayer for Kingdom Reformers**

**Father in the precious name of Jesus , I set my self apart to serve you with all my heart and to go wherever you send me . I will release from my mouth and from my walk every facet of your kingdom that you have placed in me. I will hold nothing back no matter the cost to me personally. I will share your kingdom with everyone that you identify to me . I shall be an uncompromising Ambassador for the kingdom of heaven here on planet earth until Jesus comes. I will love not my life unto death .
I consecrate myself to you right now in the name of the Father,the Son and the Holy Spirit .**

### a. Moses - (Exodus,Leviticus,Numbers,Deuteronomy)

He was called by God even though he had a speech impediment . He was a student leader and had to learn many new things in leadership. His father-in-law Jethro taught him the wisdom of delegated leadership to manage situations effectively. The Management and Business world continues with this structure. He learns to work with the anointing of God. He learns to function with the miracles of God. He becomes the representative of God before the people. He has to rescue the rebellious people before God by standing in the gap. He never enters the promised land because of disobedience to God's specific command. He was given instruction to speak to the rock to release water instead he hit the rock twice this caused God to not allow him to enter the promised land which was the reason he had been called. Moses achieved much in character development but missed the mark of integrity and accurately obeying God's instruction to him. God had much grace upon Moses and blessed his life even though he didn't achieve the fullness of his mission. Not fully obeying God is very costly and only partial blessing follows. This is a very important point for all reformers to consider.

### b. Joshua - (Deuteronomy,Joshua)

This is a young man who is given a great commission by God to take over a promise that had yet to be fulfilled. Moses had not completed the task that was given to him to possess and occupy the promised land of Canaan. Joshua rose to the challenge with absolute faith and trust in God and His methods and ways. He obtained strength form God and did not depend upon his own strength. That's a good place to be as a Christian leader and reformer. Staying faithful to the ways of God in being sanctified before entering the new land upheld the ancient divine pattern for the priesthood. Joshua had many challenges and opportunities to trust his own judgement and apply his own experience of battle tactics. He chose to obey God in all his ways. This proved to be the success of his mission. God's ways are not always easy top understand and they may totally different from the environment we live in . Nevertheless they are God's ways and plans and they will work when obeyed explicitly. Reformers must follow the plan of God and not try their own plan. God always knows best !

c. **Abraham - (Genesis 12 - 15)**

A great man of faith who received the call from God to go out of his own country and familiar settings including riches and possessions. Abraham was a rich business man . He believe God and began the journey to the promised land of modern day Israel . He learned that he had to be specifically obedient to God and received some problems because of his disobedience. However he learned from these mistakes and moves on in the call. He has faith to believe in a supernatural birth of Isaac. This was hard considering his wife Sarah had caused him some hurdles to cross over. He had been persuaded to submit to her own plan of having a child through her hand maid Hagar. This brought about such a wrong decision that we are living with the consequence of that sin today. When eventually Isaac was born and got to the right age . God asked Abraham to sacrifice his only son . Abraham obeyed God to the letter and reaped an eternal reward. He will obtain this eternal reward when Jesus comes back and sets up His kingdom. Reformers will almost certainly be asked by God to do something that brings discomfort and tests obedience to God's will.

d. **Joseph - (Genesis 37-50)**

Spoiled and favourite son of his father Jacob but this natural gifting did not bring him success instead it could have killed him. God had another plan for his life that would utilise his life circumstances.
He was the subject of extreme jealousy from his brothers who sold him into slavery. He was imprisoned . Doesn't sound like much success at this stage but the story isn't over. Joseph has been chosen by God to demonstrate the greatness of God in a time of famine . God directs the circumstances of Joseph every step of the way. During his slavery he holds himself with dignity and he is chosen by Potiphar ,a high ranking official of the Pharoah , to serve in his household. Being in the Potiphar's household was not without it's problems. Potiphar's wife takes a shine to Joseph but he remains faithful to his God.

Accused of infidelity he is imprisoned for 3 years .
Here his faith is strengthened and his reliance upon God brings forth his eventual release .
He goes from serving Potiphar's house to becoming the prime minister.

God releases his wisdom in Joseph and he stores up a great harvest in time of plenty in order to have stocks to feed the people in time of famine. God demonstrates that reliance upon him brings miraculous solutions when disaster seems the only conclusion . He officiates over the distribution of corn and meets his older brothers again but they did not recognise him. Joseph demonstrates humility and that he has a forgiving heart . He hold no offence against them and is finally reunited with his family. Reformers have to traverse seemingly impossible situations including difficult relational issues of potential offence and personal discomfort to allow God the freedom to function for His kingdom purposes. His ways are higher than our ways !

e. **Nehemiah - (Nehemiah)**

A great restoration minister used by God to bring back into use so many things for the children of Israel. Jerusalem had been totally destroyed and all the feasts stopped. Nehemiah was a man of prayer and received a heavy burden from God to do something about the terrible demise of the city and the people. In every problem against the restoration Nehemiah trusted God and allowed Him to minister through him. Nehemiah gained great favour with the king and the queen and used this friendship to access mighty resources to restore the city of Jerusalem back to it's former glory. It was not without opposition or resistance from socalled acquaintances. Nehemiah gathered a good team around him and was a charismatic leader who was able to motivate his team by accurate release of the vision God had given him for not only the city but the restoration of the Jewish feasts. Nehemiah was also used by the Lord in the restoration of God's financial system of tithing. Battles were frequent against the enemy of restoration but through good organisation and team training the result was a great success . This was a great reforming apostle in operation. Reformers will often have great opposition from those they may have trusted. It shows that it is only God who can be trusted to direct the way forward. He will also choose the right friends for the job. Team ministry has proved to be a very successful way forward when properly organised and managed. A strong intercessory heart and an accurate prayer life makes for a very successful reformer.

## f. David - (1 Samuel, 2 Samuel, 1 Kings, 2 Kings, 1 Chronicles)

Chosen by God because of His heart towards God not because of any special physical strength.

David learned to fight on the hills as a shepherd of his father's sheep. He fought bears and wolves. He grew in faith in God and became very strong in his relationship with God. Nothing frightened him because of this relationship. It would prove to be the key to overcoming the enemy of the nation of Israel, Goliath who was physically a giant against young David a slender young man. David overcame Goliath through faith.

He was later on in life chosen to replace King Saul as the king of Israel. He had served as a minstrel for Saul in his court and was nearly killed by Saul's anger and jealousy. God preserved him for greater things ahead.

David was anointed king by Prophet Samuel and his reign was full of much fighting and victories over the enemy. David shed a lot of blood which would later be something that was held against him by God. He never built the temple he was originally given by God to build. He had a notable fall when he got involved with the wife of one of his soldiers. He caused the death of this soldier by putting him in the fiercest part of the battle. He eventually married Bathsheba and had a son. This son died however which deeply grieved him.

He did have other children including Solomon the wisest and richest man recorded in the bible.

David was honourable towards the building of the temple, he put all his resources ahead for his son Solomon to build the temple. The temple was eventually built and the beautiful outcome was that God honoured the build by coming in His manifest glory and filled the temple.

This became the forerunner of our spiritual worship today. So David left a very great legacy for us for spiritual worship. Worshipping God in spirit and truth instead of religious order.

This replaced the Mosaic form of worship by introducing the worship of God from the heart. Let's remember that David wrote most of the book of Psalms, what a wonderful song writer to God. There was great reform of worship demonstrated through the life of David.

He danced without concern of offending others, reformers will often have to do something that has the potential to offend others or bring about fear of man. All these areas have to be dismissed for the greater mission given to the reformer by God.

### g. **Deborah - (Judges 4-5)**

A judge in Israel most unusual for women to hold such an office but God had a plan for her life .
The judiciary were a male dominated vocation and it was simply that God had groomed her for such a time. The nation of Israel had no king , this was pre-exile times , and as such was in need of being mothered . Deborah was a prophetess who said nothing unless God had first spoken to her. She was married and had a particular way of releasing God's decisions over certain matters that were brought to her for counsel. As she was a woman she had to do her counsel in public and not be alone indoors with a man. General Barak was a well known military man but lacked self confidence . Deborah said to Barak that God wanted him to go against the enemy who had been terrorising the area where they lived. This was King Jabin and his army captained by Sisera.
The Lord gave to Deborah the exact time for Barak accompanied by Deborah to go up against Sisera . Deborah had already told Barak that if she were to accompany him then Barak would not be the hero but that Sisera would be killed by a woman. Barak triumphed against Sisera and his army under God's favour . Sisera fled away from his chariot and entered his friends camp whose wife was Jael. Sisera slept after being given comfort within the camp . Jael put a cloth over his head and drove a tent peg into his temple thus killing him.
The prophecy was fulfilled . A song was written proclaiming Deborah as the heroin of the hour on behalf of the nation of Israel at that time. Reformers often go against the norm of society's tradition and culture . They have a higher authority to submit to . God will always move through a yielded vessel . His kingdom purpose has priority even over what is usually accepted .

It was unheard of for a woman to be a judge , but God had need of her to demonstrate his love and compassion through her to Israel.

## h. Esther - (Esther)

Esther was born to be a queen but she didn't know it. She is captured by the Persian King along with many other prospective virgins . These were going to be pampered and undergo thorough cleansing and perfuming to make them eligible to become the queen that the king was looking for. His existing queen had behaved unbecomingly and was removed from position. Haman the kings chancellor who had gained favour through subtle means was in a very strong position. After several years Esther is eventually chosen as queen because of her beauty and personality. Esther had been brought up after her parents death by her uncle Mordecai who was a scribe in the Persian palace . He had not declared his Hebrew faith. Mordecai hears of a plot to assassinate the Persian king and it is recorded in the book of records . He was never rewarded.. Mordecai didn't like Haman and even though Haman was a high ranking officer he never saluted him or stood up .
This annoyed Haman and he planned to get rid of all the Jews in the land. The king gives Haman his ring to write letters throughout the empire to kill all the Jewish people. Mordecai learns of this plot against the Jewish people by Haman and tells Esther of it. She now has to decide whether she will stand up for her people or not . This is where the familiar text begins ..."who knows whether you have come to the kingdom for such a time as this ." Esther decides that the fate of her people was more important than her personal life. First she fasts with her own maids for 3 days before going in to the king. God is with her and the king gives her permission to enter his presence. She then proceeds to release her strategy . The strategy is to invite the king and Haman to a personal dinner which she personally arranges for them. Haman thinks all is going well after the first dinner. Esther then invites them both again to another dinner.
Haman is so happy and boasts to his wife and family of his great fortune of special treatment by the queen. However he is upset when he again sees Mordecai and does not receive an acknowledgment of his rank. He complains to his wife and she suggests that he build a gallows to hang Mordecai upon. King Ahasuerus could not sleep that night and asks for the book of records to be brought before the king and be read.
Mordecai's record that he protected the king by telling about the plot against the king's life by two of his servants.

The king asks if anything has been done for Mordecai. He asks Haman who was in his court to see him what should be done for someone who should be honoured. Haman thinks it was for him and so says that the king's apparel, his crown should be put on the person and be led through the city on the king's horse. To Haman's horror, he now has to do what he has just said not for himself but for Mordecai. The next day he attends the second banquet of queen Esther. She nows tells the king of the plight of her people. She tells of the plot to kill her people by Haman. The king goes into the garden to cool off and Haman pleads for his life with queen Esther but does it by laying on her bed. The king comes back and judges that Haman is trying to be familiar with his wife.

This is Haman's end.

The gallows that was made for Mordecai is described to the king. The king give order for Haman to hung upon the gallows. The king now gives order for the Jews to form themselves into groups to fight against those who would come to kill them. The Jews overcome all their enemies. The feast of Purim is instituted. Esther as a great reformer had to decide between her own life or the lives of her people. Reformers are fully committed to the call of God upon their lives and are uncompromising in their purpose for what God puts in their heart.

### i.   Ruth - (Ruth)

Ruth joins herself to her mother in law Naomi after they have endured a great family loss of husbands and sons. Ruth's sister in law returns to her native Moab and her gods but Ruth remains with Naomi. She now makes a strong declaration " entreat me not to leave you, or to return from following after you ; for wherever you go, I will go; and where you live, I will live: your people will be my people, and your God my God: where you die, I will die, and there be buried: the Lord do so to me, and more also, If anything but death part you and me." Naomi is convinced of Ruth's determination and commitment to stay with her. They both return to Naomi's homeland of Judah and enter Bethlehem where Naomi's husband comes from. Boaz, a rich landowner and a family member of Naomi's husband Elimelech now shows kindness to Ruth. She asks him why she has found grace in his eyes seeing she is a stranger.

He tells her that he has heard about how she treated her mother in law, how she has left her family and her land and joined herself to the people of this land that you did not know. The Lord recompense your work, and a full reward be given you of the Lord God of Israel, under whose wings you are come to trust. Ruth is given continued favour to glean among the barley field with the hand maids of Boaz. She continues until the end of the barley harvest and stays with Naomi. Boaz redeems the land of Elimelech and his sons so that there would be an inheritance and that the name of the deceased family would continue. Boaz now marries Ruth and she bears a son called Obed. The women who helped at the birth now make an extraordinary statement to Naomi " Blessed be the LORD, which hath not left thee this day without a kinsman, that his name may be famous in Israel. And he shall be unto thee a restorer of thy life, and a nourisher of thine old age: for thy daughter in law, which loveth thee, which is better to thee than seven sons, hath born him." Naomi now becomes a nurse to baby Obed. This is part of the famous family line of David king of Israel and our Lord Jesus Christ. That's real honour by God for faithfulness. This is true reformer character in action. Commitment, faithfulness, tenacity and sheer hard work. Ruth is rewarded for her absolute commitment to join herself not only to her mother in law Naomi but to her people and her God. God surely rewards such character. This principle continues on today in the life of any reformer. Labour on behalf of another and a reward will come forth to your own account. This is the principle of sowing and reaping.

**Galatians 6:9.**

**"And let us not be weary in well doing: for in due season we shall reap, if we faint not."**

## j. Elijah - (1 Kings, 2 Kings)

Elijah a mighty prophet of God. God used him to release great miracles in the land of Samaria during a time when there had been no rain for several years. He is sent to King Ahab to tell him that God will demonstrate to all the people that the God of Abraham,Isaac and Israel is the true God . Elijah tells Ahab to gather the people of Israel , his 450 Prophets of Baal and the 400 prophets of the groves who sit at Jezebel's table to Mount Carmel .Elijah says they must choose between God or Baal .He instructs Ahab to sacrifice a bullock and lay it upon wood but don't light the fire. He then instructs the prophets of Baal and Jezebel's prophets to call out to their god Baal to set the sacrifice on fire. They do this all day and even cut themselves but their god does not answer . Elijah taunts them . He now stands before the people and repairs the broken altar of the Lord . He builds an altar in the name of the Lord with twelve stones representing the twelve tribes of Israel . He digs a trench around the altar and places wood upon it and lays the burnt offering upon it .
He now instructs for four barrels of water to be poured over the whole altar three times . The water now ran around the altar and he filled the trench with water. Elijah cries out to God ,

**" LORD , God of Abraham, Isaac, and of Israel, let it be known this day that thou art God in**
**Israel, and that I am thy servant, and that I have done all these things at thy word. Hear me, O LORD, hear me, that this people may know that thou art the LORD God, and that thou hast turned their heart back again."**

Fire fell from heaven and consumed the sacrifice , and the wood , and the stones and the dust and licked up the water that was in the trench. The people were astonished and fell on their faces and said " The LORD , he is the God . Elijah then instructs the prophets of baal to be taken to the brook Kishon andthere he slaughtered them all. Now Elijah tells king Ahab to get up and eat for there is an abundance of rain. Elijah goes to the top of Mount Carmel and lays upon the ground with his face between his knees. He instructs his servant to look in the sky towards the sea . He instructs him to go seven times and finally a little cloud is seen .

Now he tells Ahab to get in his chariot and go down the mountain for the rain is coming and will stop him. The hand of the LORD was on Elijah and he now girds his loins and raced down the mountain ahead of Ahab into the entrance of Jezreel.

This distance was about twenty miles . Now a surprising turn of events occurs , after Ahab tells his wife Jezebel what has happened . She threatens him with his life . He takes serious her threat and looses all his confidence and goes and hides himself in a cave . He makes negative confessions that he is no better than his fathers and asks the LORD to take his life. He is the only prophet left. Of course God has thousands of prophets elsewhere but Elijah didn't know this. God sends an angel to feed Elijah to sustain him for the forty day and night journey to Mount Horeb , the mount of God. He now stayed in a cave and the word of the Lord came to him and God asked what was he doing there ? He declares that he is the only prophet left and they are after his life. God tells him to go up the mountain and the Lord passed by . A mighty rock breaking wind , an earthquake and a fire all came and went but the Lord was not in them . He was in a still small voice and Elijah heard it. He now begins the process of passing on his mantle to Elisha. He is eventually taken up in a chariot of fire and Elisha receives the double anointing from Elijah as he was able to see him go up in the clouds. Elijah represents a particular type of reformer . When he stayed close to God many mighty miracles passed through his hands . Yet even after such great miracles he allowed himself to fear man and to doubt that God was with him.

Confidence in God is paramount for a reformer as there will many situations that threaten self confidence . God vindicated him and looked after him . Elijah demonstrates a very human reformer who could easily be an extreme working prophet of God and the next moment be carnal. This is a very real situation that faces any reformer and staying dependent upon God is the answer.

k. **Paul - ( Acts 13 18, Romans , 1 Corinthians , 2 Corinthians, Galatians , Ephesians ,
   Philippians , Colossians , 1 Thessalonians , 2 Thessalonians , 1 Timothy , 2 Timothy , Titus , Philamon , 2 Peter )**

Paul , the very well known Apostle who wrote many of the books in the New Testament . He gave guidance on leadership , church government , Christian mission , the family and marriage to name but a few. Paul ministered into these areas by means of letters that he wrote to the churches in Asia Minor such as Ephesus , Colosse , Corinth , Galatia, Philippi , Rome and Thessalonica . He also wrote more personal letters which are for our edification . These were to his spiritual family and ministerial friends such as Timothy ,Titus and Philemon. Paul epitomises the function of the New testament Apostle and laid down the way ahead for the Church to follow. He describes the structure and foundation of the Church and the government that must be in place to accurately minister the Gospel of the Kingdom. He was born a Hebrew of the tribe of Benjamin and a Pharisee . Before his conversion he was known as Saul . His conversion took place on the road to Damascus where he met the resurrected Christ and was instantly converted by the Lord. From this point he became a zealot for Christ and the Church instead of a zealot against the Church. This was total transformation and demonstrates the kind of conversion necessary for someone to undergo the later difficulties he would face. 2 Corinthians 11:21-33 records what Paul said about himself .
This was to demonstrate the suffering that goes with the office.

" *I speak as concerning reproach, as though we had been weak. Howbeit whereinsoever any is bold, (I speak foolishly,) I am bold also. Are they Hebrews? so am I. Are they Israelites? so am I. Are they the seed of Abraham? so am I. Are they ministers of Christ? (I speak as a fool) I am more; in labours more abundant, in stripes above measure, in prisons more frequent, in deaths oft.Of the Jews five times received I forty stripes save one. Thrice was I beaten with rods, once was I stoned, thrice I suffered shipwreck, a night and a day I have been in the deep; In journeyings often, in perils of waters, in perils of robbers, in perils by mine own countrymen, in perils by the heathen, in perils in the city, in perils in the wilderness, in perils in the sea, in perils among false brethren;In weariness and painfulness, in watchings often, in hunger and thirst, in fastings often, in cold and nakedness.*

*Beside those things that are without, that which cometh upon me daily, the care of all the churches. Who is weak, and I am not weak? who is offended, and I burn not? If I must needs glory, I will glory of the things which concern mine infirmities.*
*The God and Father of our Lord Jesus Christ, which is blessed for evermore, knoweth that I lie not. In Damascus the governor under Aretas the king kept the city of the damascenes with a garrison, desirous to apprehend me: And through a window in a basket was I let down by the wall, and escaped his hands."*

So we see here a comprehensive record of the suffering that follows a reformer. This doesn't mean to say all reformers will suffer these things but it is assured that following Christ will produce suffering but what great joy is the eternal result. Better to suffer for righteousness than to suffer for foolishness and carnality.

1. <u>Stephen - (Acts 6 - 7)</u>

Stephen is the first recorded New Testament martyr. He is an ordinary believer and follower of Christ but with extraordinary faith and courage. He is described in the book of Acts chapter 6 as a man full of faith and of the Holy Ghost. He was full of faith and power and did great wonders and miracles among the people. This stirred up the religious spirits that worked through the members of the synagogue, Cyrenians, Alexandrians and Cilicia and of Asia. They began to dispute with Stephen and his teaching. They set up false accusation against him and accused him of blaspheming the law of Moses and the temple. This is what the bible records of the accusation

*" For we have heard him say, that this Jesus of Nazareth shall destroy this place, and shall change the customs which Moses delivered us."*

Reformation is all about changing customs, tradition and culture to align with the value system of the kingdom of God. This was the case here. Stephen then in front of the council releases a mighty apology of the word of God about Moses and the temple. He describes their character and that of their forefathers. This is what the word records in Acts 7:51-53 of Stephen's final words against them.

*"Ye stiffnecked and uncircumcised in heart and ears, ye do always resist the Holy Ghost: as your fathers did, so do ye. Which of the prophets have not your fathers persecuted? and they have slain them which shewed before of the coming of the Just One; of whom ye have been now the betrayers and murderers: Who have received the law by the disposition of angels, and have not kept it. "* Stephen was seized and stoned by the crowd . He looked up to heaven and cried out to the Lord to receive his spirit. He then kneeled down and cried with a loud voice for the Lord not to lay their sin against them . He then fell asleep. This was just one of the accounts of the persecution of the church at Jerusalem. Reformers may have to give up their lives like Stephen did by speaking out about the truth of the word of God. Reformers do not have it easy because they always travel up the road in the opposite direction of the crowd. Their function is to be in accurate partnership with God and His kingdom purposes. These do not align with the world's system and will always cause consternation , resistance to change and stir up religious spirits within individual people and organisations . Reformers are overcomers by the words of their testimony and love not their lives unto the death..Rev 12:11.

## m. Jesus - (His own words - Matthew, Mark, Luke , John , Acts , Revelation)

Jesus is the ultimate reformer and prototype leader for us all to follow. He is the king of kings and the Lord of Lords , His name is the name above every name that can be named . Jesus showed us his humanity in his 33 years upon this earth . According to Philippians chapter 2 Jesus laid aside His Godly attributes and counted it not robbery to be equal with God . He took up the assignment that God the Father had given Him .

He was to come to earth as sinless man and to take human form upon himself. This meant he had the ability to sin but chose not to. He unlike those who were born through natural birth did not take on the adamic nature . He indeed was the second Adam. The mission he undertook was to demonstrate the kingdom of God in earth by living his life with kingdom character and values. His ultimate purpose was to bring a way back to sinful man to get back into relationship with a Holy God. This is ultimate reform in action . All of the recorded activities of Jesus always demonstrate a facet of the kingdom . He is kingdom through and through .

Of course that was what He had come to earth to do. Jesus probably underwent the greatest resistance from the spirits of religion . Paul comes a close second but Jesus really demonstrates His full commitment to complete His mission to save mankind from themselves . In the garden of Gethsemane we catch a glimpse of his humanity and it is here where he asks His father if there is another way to save humanity . He of course knows there is no plan "B" . He doesn't labour the point but declares His unswerving faithfulness and obedience to the will of God above His own will. That's greatness in the kingdom ! As we look through the different accounts of Jesus in His earthly ministry we see how he handles his disciples and the crowds that follow him. He is charismatic but wise in his manner and ways. He is careful to demonstrate the kingdom heart that is within him. This is no ordinary man but the ultimate man of God demonstrating another kingdom , a higher superior kingdom. We only need to study Jesus in the New Testament to observe kingdom in action . He is compassionate to the infirm and the elderly but strict to the spiritual forces behind sickness and disease.

He has already shown His superiority even in human form against the powers of darkness as he deals righteously with the devil . The Mount of temptation is the place where Jesus overcomes the enemy with the word of God. "It is written " For all the temptations of the flesh he overcomes them with the word.

He shows us all how we should do the same. He healed the sick and caste out devils from demonised people. He demonstrated the power of the Holy Spirit in the life of the believer. We must emulate Jesus if we are to accurately live in kingdom ways. This is our portion as reformers to show forth the ways of Christ who is in us. As His ambassadors we have become ambassadors for the kingdom of God .
Jesus is the king of the kingdom .

The principle of the word of God is this that the character of the kingdom follows the character of the king . So as we study Jesus life and do what He showed us and his teachings we will be equipped to be accurate partners of God for kingdom purpose and advance.
**1 Corinthians 2:16** tells us that we have the mind of Christ. We have the ability to access kingdom value and kingdom wisdom that leads to kingdom decision about any situation . That is the mind of Christ and the thinking process for kingdom purpose.

We submit to the Lord above our own carnal minds. This enables us to function as effective ministers of the kingdom. Jesus has given us the ultimate mandate of the kingdom to complete . This came as the great commission .

*Matthew 28:18-20*

*" And Jesus came and spake unto them, saying, All power is given unto me in heaven and in earth. Go ye therefore, and teach all nations, baptizing them in the name of the Father, and of the Son, and of the Holy Ghost:Teaching them to observe all things whatsoever I have commanded you: and, lo, I am with you always, even unto the end of the world. Amen."*

**G. Kingdom Ways , Keys and Principles**

1. All that are related to God Almighty through Jesus Christ are reformers . That situation is already a fact .Our purpose is to function effectively as citizens of the kingdom of heaven here on planet earth .We hasten Christ's return as we function this way going from one level of influence to the next . We are resourced by God in wisdom giving us strategies that propel us forward to resolve life situations . Resources can be financial or strategic . Individual or corporate . **Ephesians 4:16** gives us a very good functional statement of our structure and activity as kingdom believers and reformers of the nations .

*"For because of Him the whole body (the church, in all its various parts), closely joined and firmly knit together by the joints and ligaments with which it is supplied, when each part [with power adapted to its need] is working properly [in all its functions], grows to full maturity, building itself up in love." (Amplified version)*

As a team working together and developing greater product together than alone ; this is synergy in action.

2. The manner in which we order and behave ourselves in any situation are manners or ways .These become the ways that we live . They can be ways that manifest kingdom principles rather than earthly behaviour . Straight away there is a battle that begins in our thinking and then flows to our bodies in action . The success of our accurate representation of kingdom ways depends upon our growing relationship with the king . For us to follow Him we need to know Him better . This means spending quality time with Him and His word. It's a lot easier trying to mimic someone you know than someone you have only recently met. Our function as reformers is to emulate or copy Jesus and His ways.

These are kingdom ways !
***Kingdom ways are the inner workings of an outer manifestation.***

They are the outworking of the inner foundation that has been received. A key word in our growth as kingdom people is "revelation " .

*Revelation ( Greek - apokalupsis )*
*- to take the cover off , disclose , act of revealing , appearance , coming , enlighten.*
*" To bring forth a disclosure and revealing of something that gives greater illumination of it's detail and function"*

The level of revelation we *receive* and *assimilate* into our actions becomes the *limiting factor* of our *present demonstration* . This applies to any subject but certainly applies to our revelation and understanding of the kingdom of God. How does revelation come and how do we increase it ?

**Psalm 119:130 (Amplified Bible)**

**"The entrance and unfolding of Your words give light; their unfolding gives understanding (discernment and comprehension) to the simple. "**

**Proverbs 1:6 (Amplified Bible)**

**"That people may understand a proverb and a figure of speech or an enigma with its interpretation, and the words of the wise and their dark sayings or riddles."**

**Proverbs 1:23 (Amplified Bible)**

"If you will turn (repent) and give heed to my reproof, behold, I [Wisdom] will pour out my spirit upon you, I will make my words known to you."

**Proverbs 4:4 (Amplified Bible)**

"He taught me and said to me, Let your heart hold fast my words; keep my commandments and live."

**Isaiah 55:11 (Amplified Bible)**

"So shall My word be that goes forth out of My mouth: it shall not return to Me void [without producing any effect, useless], but it shall accomplish that which I please and purpose, and it shall prosper in the thing for which I sent it."

**Jeremiah 1:9 (Amplified Bible)**

"Then the Lord put forth His hand and touched my mouth. And the Lord said to me, Behold, I have put My words in your mouth."

All these scriptures give us helpful supplementary information to answer our question about how revelation comes and how it can increase. In all of these texts we can see that it is the function of His word that is the activating factor.

*Word ( Hebrew - dabar) - that which was spoken , decree, commandment, deed, duty, judgment, language, message, oracle, power, promise, provision, report, appoint, name, rehearse, pronounce, teach, utter.*

As we can see from the list of associated activities that function within " the word " that a required action must take place by those accessing the word if they are to benefit from this relationship . In other words if we want to grow and increase in revelation we have to input "the word" into our lives.

## 3. Healthy Food for Healthy Living

This activity of input is like feeding and it has to take place regularly just like meal breaks ! So to feed the healthy body we need healthy food .

For a healthy spiritual life we need a regular diet of "the word "

**1 Peter 2:2 (Amplified Bible)**

**"Like newborn babies you should crave (thirst for, earnestly desire) the pure (unadulterated) spiritual milk, that by it you may be nurtured and grow unto [completed] salvation,It is a simple truth that can be easily performed but it takes a decision and discipline to keep up this healthy strategy ."**

**Hebrews 5:14 (Amplified Bible)**

**"But solid food is for full-grown men, for those whose senses and mental faculties are trained by practice to discriminate and distinguish between what is morally good and noble and what is evil and contrary either to divine or human law."**

If we take this to a higher level and now consider the word as "The Word " we go from what God has said to the person of "The Word " Himself. That's a different thing altogether .
Now it becomes personal !

From dabar to Logos !

## 4. Relationship Rules !

This in itself is a transition from the level of relationship we have at present to the level we can access if we take time , prioritise time and make time ! The relationship is already set by God but it is up to the individual family member to increase access for increased intimacy . There is a law of relationship that affects our level of demonstration of kingdom . The closer we get to the king the greater potential for kingdom demonstration in and through our lives.

## 5. The Kingdom Mind

The more we focus upon the kingdom the greater the kingdom possesses our mind.
These are short truths that have revolutionary affect upon our life. Unless we are serious about the kingdom of God we cannot function effectively as kingdom citizens. We have to live and breath "kingdom " in order to function right .

**Romans 12:2 (Amplified Bible)**

**"Do not be conformed to this world (this age), [fashioned after and adapted to its external, superficial customs], but be transformed (changed) by the [entire] renewal of your mind [by its new ideals and its new attitude], so that you may prove [for yourselves] what is the good and acceptable and perfect will of God, even the thing which is good and acceptable and perfect [in His sight for you]."**

After all that's how the designer designed us ! "Kingdom First" is the order of the day .
Kingdom First doesn't mean the kingdom then other things it means kingdom first and last .
The king of the kingdom is the first and the last !

6. When we become kings we are then qualified to help those outside the kingdom , those in the world , to get into the kingdom that they are seeking . They are not aware that this seeking mode has been placed in them by God Almighty , the creator and designer .
As kings we steward the resources of the kingdom here on earth as it is in heaven .

**Genesis 1:28 (Amplified Bible)**

**"And God blessed them and said to them, Be fruitful, multiply, and fill the earth, and subdue it [using all its vast resources in the service of God and man]; and have dominion over the fish of the sea, the birds of the air, and over every living creature that moves upon the earth."**

7. As priests of righteousness we are positioned to access kingdom prosperity. A very significant scripture underlines the way which resources follow the right focus and right relationship .

**Matthew 6:33 (Amplified Bible)**
**"But seek (aim at and strive after) first of all His kingdom and His righteousness (His way of doing and being right), and then all these things taken together will be given you besides."**

Righteous means - right positioning - correct alignment with the ruling government

Kingdom provides the right to government benefits and righteousness gives the access to those benefits.
To have benefits we have to be in the kingdom but to actually receive the benefits we have to be in right standing obeying the laws of the government. The constitution of the government of the kingdom of God is the Word of God - The Holy Bible. Jesus is the King of kings and the King of the kingdom - He is the living Word and the constitution of the kingdom .

**Revelation 19:13**
**"And he was clothed with a vesture dipped in blood: and his name is called The Word of God.**
**Relationship with Jesus is essential for kingdom advancement."**

So often we see a misalignment of what God has designed. For instance religion turns God's wise design on it's head and we wonder why everything goes out of shape and has no real life. It has the appearance of divine design but does not possess the divine power .

**2 Timothy 3:5 (Amplified Bible)**
**"For [although] they hold a form of piety (true religion), they deny and reject and are strangers to the power of it [their conduct belies the genuineness of their profession]. Avoid [all] such people [turn away from them]."**

## 8. Kingdom - Righteousness relationship

Here's what it looks like as compared with the original design :
Religion = kingdom in vertical relationship i.e. power over people and righteousness in a horizontal relationship where religion drives position over people in a hierarchy of self righteousness.

The true design is this :
**Kingdom** is **HORIZONTAL** dealing with **POWER** and **Righteousness** is **VERTICAL** dealing with **POSITION** .

That's seen so clearly in Jesus' motives in **Phil.2:6,7**

**Philippians 2:6-7 (Amplified Bible)**
" Who, although being essentially one with God and in the form of God [possessing the fullness of the attributes which make God God], did not think this equality with God was a thing to be eagerly grasped or retained, but stripped Himself [of all privileges and rightful dignity], so as to assume the guise of a servant (slave), in that He became like men and was born a human being. "

**Revelation 1:8 (Amplified Bible)**

"I am the Alpha and the Omega, the Beginning and the End, says the Lord God, He Who is and Who was and Who is to come, the Almighty (the Ruler of all)"

So many are looking for answers in the world for what has a spiritual answer . The kingdom of God is what we all looking for . Not until we are joined back to God through Jesus Christ - The King , can we become kings in the kingdom . Indeed we become kings and priests .
**Revelation 5:10 (Amplified Bible)**

"And You have made them a kingdom (royal race) and priests to our God, and they shall reign [as kings] over the earth! "

## H. Kingdom Principles from Kingdom Reformers

### a. Moses - Apostle of Release
Moses achieved much in character development but missed the mark of integrity and accurately obeying God's instruction to him. God had much grace upon Moses and blessed his life even though he didn't achieve the fullness of his mission. Moses success however was due to him surrendering himself to God.
Not accurately obeying God is very costly and only partial blessing follows. This is a very important point for all reformers to consider.

### b. Joshua - Apostle of Transition
God's ways are not always easy top understand and they may totally different from the environment we live in . Nevertheless they are God's ways and plans and they will work when obeyed explicitly. Reformers must follow the plan of God and not try their own plan. God always knows best !

### c. Abraham - Foundational Apostle
Abraham obeyed God to the letter and reaped an eternal reward. He will obtain this eternal reward when Jesus comes back and sets up His kingdom. Reformers will almost certainly be asked by God to do something that brings discomfort and tests obedience to God's will.

### d. Joseph - Marketplace Apostle
Reformers have to traverse seemingly impossible situations including difficult relational issues of potential offence and personal discomfort to allow God the freedom to function for His kingdom purposes. His ways are higher than our ways !

### e. Nehemiah - Restoration Apostle of Prayer
This was a great reforming apostle in operation. Reformers will often have great opposition from those they may have trusted. It shows that it is only God who can be trusted to direct the way forward. He will also choose the right friends for the job. Team ministry has proved to be a very successful way forward when properly organised and managed. A strong intercessory heart and an accurate prayer life makes for a very successful reformer.

### f. David - Worship Apostle
There was great reform of worship demonstrated through the life of David. He danced without concern of offending others, reformers will often have to do something that has the potential to offend others or bring about fear of man. All these areas have to be dismissed for the greater mission given to the reformer by God.

### g. Deborah - Apostolic Prophet
Reformers often go against the norm of society's tradition and culture. They have a higher authority to submit to. God will always move through a yielded vessel. His kingdom purpose has priority even over what is usually accepted. It was unheard of for a woman to be a judge, but God had need of her to demonstrate his love and compassion through her to Israel.

### h. Esther - Apostle of Release
Esther as a great reformer had to decide between her own life or the lives of her people. Reformers are fully committed to the call of God upon their lives and are uncompromising in their purpose for what God puts in their heart.

### i. Ruth -
This is true reformer character in action. Commitment, faithfulness, tenacity and sheer hard work.
Ruth is rewarded for her absolute commitment to join herself not only to her mother in law Naomi but to her people and her God. God surely rewards such character. This principle continues on today in the life of any reformer. Labour on behalf of another and a reward will come forth to your own account.
This is the principle of sowing and reaping.

### j. Elijah - Prophet
Elijah represents a particular type of reformer. When he stayed close to God many mighty miracles passed through his hands. Yet even after such great miracles he allowed himself to fear man and to doubt that God was with him. Confidence in God is paramount for a reformer as there will many situations that threaten self confidence. God vindicated him and looked after him. Elijah demonstrates a very human reformer who could easily be an extreme working prophet of God and the next moment be carnal. This is a very real
situation that faces any reformer and staying dependent upon God is the answer.

### k. Paul - Prophet/Apostle
So we see here a comprehensive record of the suffering that follows a reformer . This doesn't mean to say all reformers will suffer these things but it is assured that following Christ will produce suffering but what great joy is the eternal result. Better to suffer for righteousness than to suffer for foolishness and carnality.

### l. Stephen - Apostle
Reformers may have to give up their lives like Stephen did by speaking out about the truth of the word of God. Reformers do not have it easy because they always travel up the road in the opposite direction of the crowd. Their function is to be in accurate partnership with God and His kingdom purposes. These do not align with the world's system and will always cause consternation , resistance to change and stir up religious spirits within individual people and organisations . Reformers are overcomers by the words of their testimony and love not their lives unto the death.

### m. Jesus - Apostle, Prophet, Evangelist, Pastor, Teacher
We have the ability to access kingdom value and kingdom wisdom that leads to kingdom decision about any situation . That is the mind of Christ and the thinking process for kingdom purpose. We submit to the Lord above our own carnal minds. This enables us to function as effective ministers of the kingdom. Jesus has given us the ultimate mandate of the kingdom to complete .

# Apostolic Transition

Prayer, Life and Language - A synopsis of divine strategy that is expressed through apostolic grace to
release the change for kingdom posture and lifestyle in today's world.

## Prayer

Moving from survival mentality to overcoming, victorious mentality = Governmental Prayer
It is a mentality that has within it a "completion" attitude From a defensive posture to an offensive
posture. Becoming kingdom aware instead of self centred. It's life under "kingdom possession."
So passionate about the kingdom that nothing else matters anymore!
We grow in greater revelation of "team" and "body" mindedness - this will show in relationship building the beginnings of true synergy i.e. greater things achieved through a team working together than individuals working alone.

**Eph.4:16 " From whom the whole body fitly joined together and compacted by that which every joint supplieth, according to the effectual working in the measure of every part, maketh increase of the body unto edifying of itself in love ."**

## Today's Reformation

It is global - acceptance of church apostles operating in strong impartation and revelatory ministry.
It is inward in direction - to the hearts of man. It touches everyone and everything - through all levels all
strata of society. It starts with the church community then as they are transformed and activated and released they impact the world around. Confidence in Christ is reawakened - we move with Him in a
newly inspired way seeing Acts 3:21 being fulfilled.

### Acts 3:21 (Amplified Bible)

**"Whom heaven must receive [and retain] until the time for the complete restoration of all that God spoke by the mouth of all His holy prophets for ages past [from the most ancient time in the memory of man]."**

We are in working partnership (real covenant) with Christ. This move embraces the past truths and lifts them to a new level of function.

## Worship

We never lose the inner spirit of adoration but we move under the Holy Spirit's direction into a " conquering" posture . It's not aggressive but boldly confident in Christ . We become courageous and accurate proclaimers - speaking out and singing out the promises of God . He moves through us to accomplish His purposes within this reformation move . From "bless me " to "martyrdom" !
King David is a good example of someone who was not afraid to step into a new posture of worship . He demonstrates the courage and selfless heart required to step into the spiritual worship that was being called for. His wife Michal however demonstrated the rigid religious attitude that opposes change .
It is a spectator and judgmental spirit in operation .
**1 Chron.15:27 - 29.**

## Apostolic Relationships

True spiritual government is being manifested in the hearts of senior pastors being influenced through apostolic relationships i.e. networks and conferences , visiting apostles . They begin to be bolder in declaring the accurate prophetic word of the Lord for their community (church) so dealing with religious and disobedient attitudes and spirits . Saints open their hearts in a deeper more intimate way - God's government now moves from within to manifest outwardly bringing spiritual balance in lives and allowing God to further His purposes .

## Transition
Like the pillar of fire by night and the cloud by day as the Israelites in the wilderness , we too have to follow the resources of God . As He moves to new positions in the spiritual realm so we follow . This is known as our journeying or migration .To be aligned with God and be able to partake of His resources for this hour we must follow Him where He is ! The king will always provide for His kingdom citizens because that's a benefit of a righteous kingdom. Righteous citizens are always in right positioning with the king and His kingdom. Relationship is built upon righteous activity .

**Exodus 40:38 " For the cloud of the Lord was upon the tabernacle by day , and fire was on it by night , in the sight of all the house of Israel , throughout all their journeys ."**

**Apostolic Grace**

"Let my people go" Moses spoke to Pharoah to release the Israelites - This impartation empowered the release. Today Apostolic Grace empowers the people to come out of bondage and to take up bold new positions in the spirit. Divine order is being accomplished. This is a grand plan of God that we are honoured to partake with Him. The price is the massive transformation within us which is also massive in scale i.e. how many it affects ! Within this grace are invested the following :Faith, wisdom, understanding, knowledge, courage, leadership, ability and prophetic discernment.
**2 John 1:3** is our foundational scripture that embraces these truths.
**" Grace (unmerited favour and supernatural ability) be with you (firmly attached as one) mercy (active compassion) and peace (shalom, well-being in all realms of living) from God the Father (apostolic authority) and from the Lord Jesus Christ, the son of the Father (correct and accurate reproduction and authority level) in truth (total absence of falsity) and love ( agape, God's love, sacrificial and selfless - the heart of martyrdom.) "**
**New Concepts of Church (assembly)**
The church without walls - greater works in the community than within the church building. Reaching out to the poor, the orphans and widows so that we become the answer to their need. When we minister to the needy we minister to the Lord. From temple ministry focus to community, marketplace and " nations " focus. We're breaking out with a newly ignited heart for God's purposes - to redeem the lost the prodigal sons ! Renewed understanding of kingdom purpose. Being possessed by the kingdom.
Kingdom first in all things.

**Right Food**
Like any good army, we too have to get the right food ! As all the other reformation moves of God this apostolic reformation has within it revealed truth from the Holy Spirit. This has impacted the hearts of pioneer ministers who write material for others to feed upon and receive what God requires from us.
We are open to this move and all other subsequent moves. We receive certain equipping by feasting
upon the Holy Spirit directed material.

## Right Company

Joining with others within apostolic networks and receiving apostolic grace to " run the race "
= relational influence .Apostles minister into our assemblies = transitional influence.
Attending conferences and reading books on the apostolic = temporary influence.

**Prov.13:20**
**" He that walketh with wise men shall be wise : but a companion of fools shall be destroyed ."**

## Intercession

As we line up with the Lord and pray into our assemblies . He will ensure that they have the opportunity to come in line with His present move . Some may not however but like all His sons they are still loved by Him . They just are not in the place He wants them to be . We continue in steadfast prayer and belief . We continue to change - change breeds change . Change also causes conflict . Natural man is always against something he does know anything about ! He hates change .We have to be continuously transformed to enable our appreciation of change and then work with it .

## Restitution of all things - Christ released from heaven

This present apostolic move of God is crucial to the fulfilling of this scripture . Let us walk out our lives with renewed vision, greater determination and boldness to complete our mission . Christ's return will be enabled .Let's see it done in Jesus name .Amen and amen ! The Spirit and the bride say come !!

**Rev.22:17 " And the Spirit and the bride say , Come . And let him that heareth say , Come . And let him that is athirst come . And whosoever will , let him take the water of life freely."**

# Reformation of the Nations
## (Manual for Kingdom Advance)

We firmly believe in the kingdom principle of reproduction and multiplication that comes forth from the impartation received during the release of this manual.

It is our desire that all who have received this teaching honour the spirit in which this manual has been made available to the body of Christ in the nations.

We would like every person who purchases this manual to register on the form overleaf to help us keep track of where the manual is being released.

For those who register we give permission to reproduce this manual for personal use and for training the body of Christ.

Please also use the address below to inform us of your testimonies and/or inform us of any recommendations you may have regarding the manual.

Please return the registration details to:

| In the Philippines | Other Regions |
| --- | --- |
| Tehillah Apostolic Network Inc. | Tehillah Apostolic Network |
| 39 Begonia Street | 25 Cotswold Gardens |
| Tahanan Village | East Ham |
| Parañaque City | London E6 3HZ |
| Philippines 1700 | United Kingdom |
| Email:aecphil@tannet.asia | tannetwork@gmail.com |

# Reformation of the Nations
(Manual for Kingdom Advance)

## Registration Form

Name : _____

Address : _____

_____

Ministry/Church : _____

Email: _____

Comments _____

_____

_____

_____

_____

_____

_____

Date : _____

Photocopy this page and complete and send to the relevant address overleaf.

The Apostolic Equipping Center has been formed to provide kingdom training to the body of Christ in the nations.

We publish below a brief overview of our training curriculum: Please refer to contact details below to arrange training.

## Present Courses

- School of Worship
- Apostolic Training
- Prophetic Schools
- Governmental Prayer
- Reforming the Nations
- Watchman Intercessor School
- Ministering Spiritual Gifts (MSG)
- Restoring the Foundations (RTF)

Apostolic Equipping Center (AECPhil.)

A ministry of
Tehillah Apostolic Network Inc.
(SEC Phil.)Co. Reg. No.CN200310358

Reg.Office:
39 Begonia Street
Tahanan Village
Parañaque City
Tel/Fax:(00632)8427957

For more information please contact Admin Dept
Rev.Aby Tan
(AEC Phil - Administrator - Senior Tutor)
Philippines

Tel:#+639265243781

Email:aecphil@tannet.asia
Internet:www.tannet.asia

www.ingramcontent.com/pod-product-compliance
Lightning Source LLC
Chambersburg PA
CBHW051718040426
42446CB00008B/946